THE DOORWAY TO YOUR SUCCESS WITH ARTIFICIAL INTELLIGENCE

By. Dr. Demoine Kinney

The Doorway to Your Success with Artificial Intelligence

By Dr. Demoine Kinney

Printed in the United States

ISBN: 978-1-953760-42-5 Paperback

Dedication

I first would like to Thank God my father for giving me the mind to want to help people since I was a little boy but had no idea that my life would be so full of receiving and pouring out. I would like to thank my Lord and savior Jesus Christ for teaching me how to live and serve the way he did when he walked the face of this earth.

I would like to dedicate this book to my family which includes my beautiful wife Dr. Marita Kinney, our 6 children Jermaine, Jerney, Tahj, Anisa, Shiloh and Shay for always loving and believing in me. I would like to thank my mom for always being their for me and believing in my dreams. I would like to thank my siblings for always reminding me of what is important in life and all of my Grandparents for reminding me daily that they have my back and how much my ancestors went through for me to be here now.

To my Uncles, Aunts, Cousins, Friends and Colleagues thank you all for the support and the motivation to play bigger and reminding me to never dim my light for anyone or anything. Last but not least I would like to thank my partners The Global Black Economic Forum, The Academy of Advancing Excellence and Essence for the amazing opportunities that you all have given me to coach, speak and network with some of the worlds greatest minds. I pray this book makes you all proud as well.

Thank you all and I pray that this book is not only informational but also a blessing to all that will read it.

Peace and Blessings to You all,

Dr. Arthur Demoine Kinney

Table of Content

Introduction

By The United Global AI Equity Alliance Inc.

Welcome to The Doorway of Your Success with Artificial Intelligence (AI)! In this book, Dr. Demoine Kinney, an internationally recognized expert in the fields of Artificial intelligence, Cryptocurrency, Blockchain, Business Development, Compliance, Education and Training, Government Contracting, Program/Project Management, Quality Assurance, provides a comprehensive and accessible guide to understanding and leveraging the power of AI to achieve personal and professional success.

Drawing on his decades of experience in academia, business, industry, military and government contracting, Dr. Kinney offers a unique and insightful perspective on the opportunities and challenges presented by AI, and provides practical strategies for harnessing its potential to drive innovation, improve efficiency, and create new business opportunities.

The Doorway to Your Success with Artificial Intelligence is divided into three parts. In Part 1, Dr. Kinney provides an overview of the basics of AI, including its history, key concepts, and applications. He explores the potential benefits and risks of AI, and discusses the ethical considerations that must be taken into account when developing and deploying AI systems.

In Part 2, Dr. Kinney delves deeper into the practical applications of AI, discussing how it can be used to improve business operations, enhance customer experiences, and drive innovation. He provides case studies and examples of successful AI implementations, and offers guidance on how to get started with AI in your own organization.

In Part 3, Dr. Kinney offers practical advice and strategies for leveraging AI to achieve personal and professional success. He discusses how to develop an AI strategy, how to build and manage an AI team, and how to navigate the ethical and regulatory challenges presented by AI. He also provides guidance on how to stay up-to-date on the latest developments in the field and how to position yourself for a successful career in AI.

Whether you are a business leader looking to harness the power of AI to drive growth and innovation, or an individual looking to build a career in AI, The Doorway to Your Success with Artificial Intelligence is an essential resource. Dr. Kinney's clear, concise, and insightful writing style, along with his extensive experience in the field, make this book an invaluable guide for anyone interested in AI. So, if you are ready to unlock the potential of AI and take your personal and professional success to the next level be sure to have something to take notes with and brace yourself for this journey to the Doorway of Your Success with Artificial Intelligence (AI).

CHAPTER 1

What is Artificial Intelligence

Artificial Intelligence (AI) is a broad and rapidly evolving field of computer science that seeks to create intelligent machines that can perform tasks that typically require human-like intelligence, such as understanding natural language, recognizing objects, making decisions, and solving complex problems. AI is a multidisciplinary field that draws on a variety of techniques and approaches from fields such as mathematics, engineering, computer science, psychology, and neuroscience.

At its core, AI is concerned with developing algorithms and models that can enable machines to learn from data and make decisions based on that data. This involves teaching machines to recognize patterns, make predictions, and take actions based on those predictions. There are many different approaches to AI, including machine learning, natural language processing, computer vision, robotics, and expert systems.

Machine learning is a subfield of AI that involves training machines to learn from data. This involves feeding large amounts of data into algorithms that can identify patterns and make predictions. Machine learning algorithms can be divided into two main categories: supervised learning and unsupervised learning. Supervised learning involves training machines to recognize patterns in labeled data, while unsupervised learning involves training machines to identify patterns in unlabeled data.

Natural language processing (NLP) is another subfield of AI that involves teaching machines to understand and generate human language. This involves developing algorithms that can analyze and process text data, such as speech, emails, and social media posts. NLP can be used for tasks such as sentiment analysis, chatbot development, and language translation.

Computer vision is another subfield of AI that involves teaching machines to recognize and interpret images and videos. This involves developing algorithms that can analyze and process visual data, such as facial recognition, object recognition, and motion detection. Computer vision can be used for tasks such as autonomous vehicles, surveillance, and augmented reality.

Robotics is another subfield of AI that involves building and programming machines to perform physical tasks. This involves developing algorithms that can enable machines to navigate and interact with their environment, such as grasping objects and manipulating them. Robotics can be used for tasks such as manufacturing, search and rescue, and healthcare.

Expert systems are another subfield of AI that involves building machines that can simulate human expertise. This involves developing algorithms that can represent human knowledge and reasoning, and enable machines to solve complex problems. Expert systems can be used for tasks such as medical diagnosis, financial analysis, and legal research.

AI has the potential to transform many industries and aspects of our lives, from healthcare and education to transportation and entertainment. It can improve efficiency, reduce costs, and create new business opportunities. However, it also raises important ethical and societal questions, such as job displacement, privacy, and security. As AI continues to evolve, it will be important to approach it with a balanced and thoughtful perspective, recognizing its potential benefits and risks.

In summary, AI is a multidisciplinary field of computer science that seeks to create intelligent machines that can perform tasks that typically require human-like intelligence. It involves developing algorithms and models that can enable machines to learn from data, make decisions based on that data, and perform complex tasks. There are many different approaches to AI, including machine learning, natural language processing, computer vision, robotics, and expert systems. AI has the potential to transform many industries and aspects of our lives, but it also raises important ethical and societal questions that must be addressed.

CHAPTER 2

The History of Artificial Intelligence (AI)

The history of Artificial Intelligence (AI) can be traced back to the early days of computing, when researchers and scientists began exploring the possibility of creating machines that could mimic human intelligence. One of the earliest examples of AI was the Logic Theorist, a program developed by Allen Newell and Herbert A. Simon in the 1950s. The Logic Theorist was able to prove mathematical theorems, demonstrating that machines could perform tasks that typically required human-like intelligence.

In the 1960s, the field of AI saw significant growth and development, with the establishment of organizations such as the Massachusetts Institute of Technology (MIT) and the

Stanford Research Institute (SRI). During this time, researchers began developing more sophisticated algorithms and models for AI, and they made significant progress in areas such as natural language processing and computer vision.

In the 1970s and 1980s, the field of AI experienced a period of decline, as researchers and investors became frustrated with the lack of progress and the high costs associated with AI research. However, in the 1990s, the field of AI saw a resurgence, driven in part by advances in computing power and the availability of large amounts of data.

In recent years, AI has seen rapid growth and development, with the emergence of deep learning and other advanced machine learning techniques. AI is now being used in a wide range of applications, from computer vision and natural language processing to predictive analytics and cybersecurity.

It's worth noting that the history of AI is not without controversy. There have been debates and disputes throughout the years about the definition of AI and the extent to which machines can truly mimic human intelligence. Some argue that AI is still in its infancy and that significant progress is still needed, while others argue that

AI has already surpassed human-like intelligence in certain areas.

In conclusion, the history of Artificial Intelligence (AI) can be traced back to the early days of computing, with significant developments and growth in the 1960s and a resurgence in the 1990s. AI has seen rapid growth and development in recent years, driven in part by advances in computing power and the availability of large amounts of data. While there have been debates and disputes about the definition of AI and the extent to which machines can mimic human intelligence, there is no doubt that AI has the potential to greatly impact our world in the coming years.

CHAPTER 3

What are Neural Networks

Neural networks are a type of machine learning algorithm that are inspired by the structure and function of the human brain. They are designed to mimic the way that neurons in the brain process information and make decisions. Neural networks consist of layers of interconnected nodes, or "neurons," that process information and pass it along to the next layer.

The basic idea behind neural networks is that they can learn to recognize patterns in data by adjusting the weights of the connections between the neurons. This is done through a process called training, which involves feeding the network large amounts of labeled data and adjusting the weights of the connections based on the errors made by the network.

The goal is to adjust the weights so that the network makes fewer errors and can correctly classify or predict the output for new, unseen data.

Neural networks can be used for a wide range of tasks, such as image and speech recognition, natural language processing, and predictive modeling. They are particularly well-suited for tasks that involve large amounts of data and complex patterns, and they have achieved state-of-the-art performance on many benchmark tasks.

There are many different types of neural networks, including feedforward networks, recurrent networks, and convolutional networks. Feedforward networks are the simplest type of neural network and consist of a series of layers that process information in one direction, from input to output. Recurrent networks, on the other hand, are capable of processing sequential data, such as time series data, and they have feedback connections that allow information to be passed back and forth between layers. Convolutional networks are a type of neural network that is specifically designed for processing images and videos, and they use filters to extract features from the data.

There are also many different architectures and training methods for neural networks, such as deep learning, transfer learning, and reinforcement learning. Deep learning is a type of neural network that consists of many layers, and it is particularly well-suited for tasks that involve large amounts of data and complex patterns. Transfer learning is a technique that involves using a pre-trained neural network as a starting point for a new task, and it can help to reduce the amount of training data and computational resources needed. Reinforcement learning is a type of machine learning that involves training an agent to take actions in an environment to maximize a reward signal, and it can be used for tasks such as autonomous vehicles and game playing.

Neural networks have many applications, including computer vision, natural language processing, speech recognition, and predictive modeling. In computer vision, neural networks can be used to recognize objects in images and videos, and they have achieved state-of-the-art performance on tasks such as image classification and object detection.

In natural language processing, neural networks can be used to analyze and process text data, such as speech and social media posts, and they can be used for tasks such as sentiment analysis and machine translation. In speech recognition, neural networks can be used to convert spoken language into text, and they have achieved state-of-the-art performance on tasks such as speech recognition and speech synthesis.

In predictive modeling, neural networks can be used to make predictions about future events based on historical data, and they have been used for tasks such as stock market prediction and weather forecasting.

Neural networks have many advantages as a machine learning algorithm. They can handle large amounts of data and complex patterns, and they can learn to recognize patterns that may not be easily apparent to humans. They can also adapt to new data and learn from it, allowing them to improve their performance over time. However, they also have some disadvantages, such as the need for large amounts of labeled data and computational resources, and the potential for overfitting, where the network learns to recognize patterns in the training data that do not generalize to new data.

Neural networks are a type of machine learning algorithm that are inspired by the structure and function of the human brain. They consist of layers of interconnected nodes that process information and make decisions based on that information. Neural networks can be used for a wide range of tasks, such as image and speech recognition, natural language processing, and predictive modeling.

They have many advantages as a machine learning algorithm, but they also have some disadvantages, such as the need for large amounts of labeled data and computational resources. Neural networks have many applications, and they have achieved state-of-the-art performance on many benchmark tasks. As computer hardware and software continue to advance, neural networks are expected to become even more powerful and widespread.

In recent years, neural networks have become increasingly popular and widely used in a variety of applications, including computer vision, natural language processing, speech recognition, and predictive modeling. This is due in part to advances in computing power and the availability of large amounts of data, which have made it possible to train more complex and powerful neural networks.

One of the key advantages of neural networks is their ability to learn from large amounts of data and identify patterns that may not be easily apparent to humans. This makes them well-suited for tasks such as image and speech recognition, where there may be many subtle differences between different objects or sounds that need to be discriminated.

Another advantage of neural networks is their ability to adapt to new data and improve their performance over time. This makes them well-suited for tasks such as predictive modeling, where the goal is to make accurate predictions about future events based on historical data.

However, neural networks also have some disadvantages. One of the main challenges with neural networks is the need for large amounts of labeled data to train them effectively. Labeled data is data that has been manually annotated or labeled with the correct output, and it is essential for training neural networks to recognize patterns and make predictions. The more labeled data that is available, the better the neural network is likely to perform.

Another challenge with neural networks is the potential for overfitting. Overfitting occurs when a neural network learns to recognize patterns in the training data that do not generalize to new data. This can result in poor performance on new, unseen data, and it is important to use techniques such as regularization and cross-validation to prevent overfitting.

Despite these challenges, neural networks have many advantages as a machine learning algorithm, and they are expected to continue to be a valuable tool for a wide range of applications. As computing power and data availability continue to increase, it is likely that neural networks will become even more powerful and widespread.

In conclusion, neural networks are a type of machine learning algorithm that are inspired by the structure and function of the human brain. They consist of layers of interconnected nodes that process information and make decisions based on that information. Neural networks can be used for a wide range of tasks, such as image and speech recognition, natural language processing, and predictive modeling.

They have many advantages as a machine learning algorithm, but they also have some disadvantages, such as the need for large amounts of labeled data and the potential for overfitting. Neural networks have many applications, and they have achieved state-of-the-art performance on many benchmark tasks. As computer hardware and software continue to advance, neural networks are expected to become even more powerful and widespread.

CHAPTER 4

The benefits and risks of AI for individuals

AI has the potential to benefit individuals in many ways, and there are many use cases where AI can help improve people's lives. Here are five examples of how AI can benefit individuals:

1. **Personalized healthcare:** AI can be used to analyze a person's genetic information, medical history, and lifestyle data to provide personalized recommendations for preventative care, treatment plans, and lifestyle changes. This can help individuals identify potential health issues before they become serious and improve their overall health and well-being.

2. Smart homes: AI can be used to create smart homes that can learn a person's preferences and habits and adjust the environment accordingly. For example, AI can be used to control temperature, lighting, and entertainment systems based on a person's schedule and preferences, and it can also help monitor for potential safety issues, such as detecting smoke or water leaks.

3. Personalized education: AI can be used to create personalized learning plans for students based on their strengths and weaknesses, and it can also provide real-time feedback and support to help them improve their performance. This can help students learn more effectively and improve their academic achievement.

4. Financial planning: AI can be used to analyze a person's financial data and provide personalized recommendations for budgeting, investing, and saving. This can help individuals make more informed financial decisions and improve their financial security.

5. Mental health support: AI can be used to provide mental health support and therapy to individuals, such as through chatbots or virtual reality therapies. This can help individuals access mental health support more easily and conveniently, and it can also help reduce the stigma associated with mental health issues.

Overall, AI has the potential to greatly improve the lives of individuals by providing personalized recommendations, support, and services. By leveraging AI, individuals can improve their health, finances, education, and mental well-being, and they can live more convenient and efficient lives.

It's worth noting that while AI has the potential to greatly benefit individuals, it's important to approach its use with caution. There are concerns about privacy and security with the collection and use of personal data, and it's important that individuals are informed about how their data is being collected and used and have control over it. Additionally, there are concerns about bias and discrimination with AI algorithms, and it's important that these issues are addressed and mitigated to ensure that AI is fair and equitable for all individuals involved.

Artificial Intelligence (AI) has the potential to greatly benefit individuals in many ways, but it also comes with risks. Listed below are a few of the risks of AI to individuals:

1. **Privacy and security:** One of the main risks of AI is the potential for breaches of privacy and security of personal information. AI systems often require

access to large amounts of personal data, and there is a risk that this data could be compromised or misused. It's important for individuals to be aware of the data that is being collected and how it is being used, and to take steps to protect their privacy.

2. **Bias and discrimination:** Another risk of AI is the potential for bias and discrimination. AI systems are trained on data, and if that data is biased or discriminatory, the AI system may also be biased or discriminatory. This can have serious consequences, such as unfair treatment or discrimination in areas such as employment and housing. It's important for individuals to be aware of the potential for bias and discrimination in AI systems, and to advocate for fair and equitable treatment.

3. **Dependence on technology:** Another risk of AI is the potential for dependence on technology. As AI systems become more sophisticated, they may replace human workers in certain tasks, leading to job displacement and unemployment. This can have serious social and economic consequences. It's important for individuals to be aware of the potential for dependence on technology, and to

consider how they can adapt and evolve in response to changing technological landscapes.

4. **Misuse of technology:** Another risk of AI is the potential for misuse of technology. AI systems can be used for malicious purposes, such as cyberattacks and propaganda, and it's important for individuals to be aware of the potential for misuse and to take steps to protect themselves.

As you can see with proper consideration and implementation, AI can be a powerful tool for improving the lives of individuals and society as a whole. By being informed and proactive, individuals can mitigate the risks of AI and ensure that they can benefit from its potential while also protecting their rights and interests. So in other words you are still needed to ensure things are accurate and accountable which solidifies the fact that humans are AI need each other to survive.

In conclusion, AI has the potential to greatly benefit individuals in many ways, from personalized healthcare and education to financial planning and mental health support. By leveraging AI, individuals can improve their lives and live more convenient and efficient lives. However, it's important to approach its use with caution and ensure that privacy, security, and fairness are prioritized.

CHAPTER 5

The benefits and risk of AI in Business

Artificial Intelligence (AI) has the potential to revolutionize the way businesses operate and compete in the marketplace. By leveraging AI, businesses can improve their operations, reduce costs, and create new revenue streams. Here are five ways that AI can benefit businesses:

1. **Improved operational efficiency:** AI can be used to automate repetitive and mundane tasks, such as data entry and data analysis, freeing up employees to focus on more strategic and value-added tasks. This can help businesses improve their operational efficiency and reduce costs. For example, AI can be used to automate the process of sorting and categorizing customer

inquiries, allowing businesses to respond more quickly and accurately to customer requests.

2. **Enhanced customer experience:** AI can be used to analyze customer data and provide personalized recommendations and experiences. This can help businesses improve customer satisfaction and loyalty, and it can also help them identify potential up selling and cross-selling opportunities. For example, AI can be used to analyze a customer's browsing and purchasing history to recommend products that they may be interested in.

3. **Improved predictive analytics:** AI can be used to analyze historical data and make predictions about future trends and events. This can help businesses make more informed decisions and improve their overall performance. For example, AI can be used to predict customer churn, allowing businesses to take proactive steps to retain customers and prevent losses.

4. **Enhanced cybersecurity:** AI can be used to detect and prevent cyber threats, such as malware and phishing attacks. This can help businesses protect their data and systems, and it can also help them respond more quickly and effectively to security incidents. For example, AI can

be used to analyze network traffic and identify unusual patterns or behaviors that may indicate a security threat.

5. **New revenue streams:** AI can be used to create new products and services that leverage its capabilities, such as chatbots and virtual assistants. This can help businesses differentiate themselves from competitors and create new revenue streams. For example, AI can be used to develop a chatbot that can provide customer support and answer frequently asked questions, reducing the need for human customer service representatives.

It's worth noting that while AI has the potential to greatly benefit businesses, it's important to approach its use with caution. There are concerns about privacy and security with the collection and use of customer data, and it's important that businesses are transparent about how they are using AI and provide customers with control over their data. Additionally, there are concerns about bias and discrimination with AI algorithms, and it's important that these issues are addressed and mitigated to ensure that AI is fair and equitable for all customers.

Artificial Intelligence (AI) has the potential to greatly benefit businesses, but it also comes with risks. Here are some of the risks of AI to businesses:

1. **Privacy and security:** One of the main risks of AI to businesses is the potential for breaches of privacy and security. AI systems often require access to large amounts of sensitive business data, and there is a risk that this data could be compromised or misused. It's important for businesses to be aware of the data that is being collected and how it is being used, and to take steps to protect their privacy and security

2. **Bias and discrimination:** Another risk of AI to businesses is the potential for bias and discrimination. AI systems are trained on data, and if that data is biased or discriminatory, the AI system may also be biased or discriminatory. This can have serious consequences, such as unfair treatment or discrimination in areas such as hiring and promotion. It's important for businesses to be aware of the potential for bias and discrimination in AI systems, and to take steps to ensure that their AI systems are fair and equitable.

3. **Dependence on technology:** Another risk of AI to businesses is the potential for dependence on

technology. As AI systems become more sophisticated, they may replace human workers in certain tasks, leading to job displacement and unemployment. This can have serious social and economic consequences. It's important for businesses to be aware of the potential for dependence on technology, and to consider how they can adapt and evolve in response to changing technological landscapes.

4. Misuse of technology: Another risk of AI to businesses is the potential for misuse of technology. AI systems can be used for malicious purposes, such as cyberattacks and intellectual property theft, and it's important for businesses to be aware of the potential for misuse and to take steps to protect themselves.

As you can see AI has the potential to greatly benefit businesses, but it also comes with risks. It's important for businesses to be aware of these risks and to take steps to protect themselves. By being informed and proactive, businesses can mitigate the risks of AI and ensure that they can benefit from its potential while also protecting their rights and interests.

In conclusion, AI has the potential to greatly benefit businesses in many ways, from improved operational efficiency and customer experience to enhanced predictive analytics and cybersecurity. By leveraging AI, businesses can improve their overall performance and create new revenue streams. However, it's important to approach its use with caution and ensure that privacy, security, and fairness are prioritized. With proper consideration and implementation, AI can be a powerful tool for improving the operations and competitiveness of businesses.

CHAPTER 6

The benefits and risk of AI in Government Contracting

Artificial Intelligence (AI) has the potential to greatly benefit government contracting, but it also comes with risks. In this chapter, we will explore the benefits and risks of using AI in government contracting, and we will provide recommendations for how to mitigate those risks and maximize the benefits.

The Benefits of using AI in government contracting include the following:

1. **Efficiency and cost savings:** One of the main benefits of using AI in government contracting is the potential for efficiency and cost savings. AI systems can automate

repetitive and time-consuming tasks, such as data entry and document review, which can save government agencies and contractors time and money. AI can also help to identify and eliminate waste and inefficiencies in government contracting processes, which can further reduce costs.

2. Improved accuracy and consistency: Another benefit of using AI in government contracting is the potential for improved accuracy and consistency. AI systems can be trained to recognize patterns and make decisions based on data, which can help to reduce errors and improve the accuracy of government contracting processes. This can be particularly important in areas such as contract administration, where errors can have serious consequences.

3. Increased transparency and accountability: AI can also help to increase transparency and accountability in government contracting. AI systems can be used to track and monitor contracting processes, which can help to identify and address issues such as corruption and fraud. This can help to build trust and confidence in government contracting processes, and it can also help to promote fairness and equity.

4. **Enhanced decision-making:** AI can also help to enhance decision-making in government contracting. AI systems can be used to analyze large amounts of data and provide insights and recommendations, which can help government agencies and contractors make better-informed decisions. This can be particularly important in areas such as procurement and project management, where data-driven decision-making can help to improve outcomes and reduce risks.

The Risks of using AI in government contracting include the following:

1. **Privacy and security:** One of the main risks of using AI in government contracting is the potential for breaches of privacy and security. AI systems often require access to large amounts of sensitive data, and there is a risk that this data could be compromised or misused. It's important for government agencies and contractors to be aware of the data that is being collected and how it is being used, and to take steps to protect their privacy and security.

2. **Bias and discrimination:** Another risk of AI to government contracting is the potential for bias and discrimination. AI systems are trained on data, and if that data is biased or discriminatory, the AI system may also

be biased or discriminatory. This can have serious consequences, such as unfair treatment or discrimination in areas such as procurement and project management. It's important for government agencies and contractors to be aware of the potential for bias and discrimination in AI systems, and to take steps to ensure that their AI systems are fair and equitable.

3. **Dependence on technology:** Another risk of AI to government contracting is the potential for dependence on technology. As AI systems become more sophisticated, they may replace human workers in certain tasks, leading to job displacement and unemployment. This can have serious social and economic consequences. It's important for government agencies and contractors to be aware of the potential for dependence on technology, and to consider how they can adapt and evolve in response to changing technological landscapes.

4. **Misuse of technology:** Another risk of AI to government contracting is the potential for misuse of technology. AI systems can be used for malicious purposes, such as cyberattacks and propaganda, and it's important for government agencies and contractors to

be aware of the potential for misuse and to take steps to protect themselves.

The Recommendations for mitigating risks and maximizing benefits are as follows:

1. **Establish clear guidelines and policies:** It's important for government agencies and contractors to establish clear guidelines and policies for the use of AI in government contracting. These guidelines should include provisions for data privacy and security, as well as for fairness and equity in AI systems.

2. **Ensure transparency and accountability:** Government agencies and contractors should ensure that AI systems are transparent and accountable, and that they are subject to regular audits and reviews. This can help to build trust and confidence in AI systems, and it can also help to identify and address issues such as corruption and fraud.

3. **Invest in education and training:** Government agencies and contractors should invest in education and training to ensure that their employees have the skills and knowledge they need to work effectively with AI systems. This can help to reduce errors and improve the accuracy of AI systems, and it can also help to ensure that

employees are equipped to adapt and evolve in response to changing technological landscapes.

4. **Foster collaboration and partnerships:** Government agencies and contractors should foster collaboration and partnerships with other organizations in the field of AI. This can help to share knowledge and resources, and it can also help to build a broader and more diverse community of AI experts and practitioners.

There are several ways in which AI can be used in government contracting to improve efficiency, accuracy, and transparency. Some examples include:

1. **Proposal evaluation:** AI can be used to analyze proposals and score them based on predefined criteria, reducing the time and effort required for manual evaluation and ensuring a fair and consistent evaluation process.

2. **Contract monitoring:** AI can be used to monitor contract performance and identify potential issues, such as delays or cost overruns, in real-time, allowing for early intervention and resolution.

3. **Compliance monitoring:** AI can be used to monitor compliance with government regulations and contract

terms, ensuring that contractors are meeting their obligations and avoiding potential penalties.

4. **Predictive analytics:** AI can be used to analyze historical data and make predictions about future trends, such as demand for certain services or potential risks, allowing for more informed decision-making.

5. **Document management:** AI can be used to automate document management and classification, reducing the time and effort required for manual document management and ensuring compliance with retention policies.

6. **Cybersecurity:** AI can be used to detect and prevent cyber attacks, protecting sensitive data and ensuring compliance with data protection regulations.

Overall, AI has the potential to significantly improve the efficiency, accuracy, and transparency of government contracting, while also reducing costs and improving the overall customer experience.

In conclusion, AI has the potential to greatly benefit government contracting, but it also comes with risks. It's important for government agencies and contractors to be aware of these risks and to take steps to mitigate them. By establishing clear guidelines and policies, ensuring transparency and accountability, investing in education and training, and fostering collaboration and partnerships, government agencies and contractors can maximize the benefits of AI while minimizing the risks.

CHAPTER 7

The use of AI in Project and Program Management

Artificial Intelligence (AI) has the potential to greatly benefit project and program management, and there are many ways that AI can be used to improve efficiency, productivity, and decision-making in project and program management. In this chapter, we will explore some of the ways that AI can be used for project and program management, and we will provide examples of how these techniques have been used in practice.

1. **Project scheduling and resource allocation:** One way that AI can be used for project and program management is in project scheduling and resource allocation. AI systems can be used to analyze historical data and forecast future

demand, which can help project and program managers to create more accurate and realistic schedules and resource allocation plans. This can help to improve efficiency and productivity, and it can also help to reduce the risk of delays and cost overruns.

For example, a construction company used an AI system to analyze historical data on project schedules and resource allocation. The AI system was able to identify trends and patterns in the data, and it was able to use this information to create more accurate and realistic schedules and resource allocation plans. As a result, the company was able to complete projects more efficiently and on time, and it was able to reduce its costs by several million dollars.

2. **Risk management:** Another way that AI can be used for project and program management is in risk management. AI systems can be used to analyze large amounts of data and identify potential risks and vulnerabilities, which can help project and program managers to take proactive steps to mitigate those risks. This can help to improve the overall success of projects and programs, and it can also help to reduce the risk of cost overruns and delays.

For example, a company that was building a new data center used an AI system to analyze potential risks and vulnerabilities. The AI system was able to identify potential threats such as power outages and cyberattacks, and it was able to provide recommendations for how the company could mitigate those risks. As a result, the company was able to complete the project on time and on budget, and it was able to minimize the risk of costly downtime.

3. Resource optimization: Another way that AI can be used for project and program management is in resource optimization. AI systems can be used to analyze data on resource usage and identify opportunities for optimization, which can help project and program managers to use their resources more efficiently and effectively. This can help to reduce costs and improve project and program outcomes.

For example, a manufacturing company used an AI system to analyze data on machine usage and production rates. The AI system was able to identify opportunities for improving efficiency, such as by adjusting production schedules to take advantage of off-peak hours. As a result, the company was able to increase its production output by 15%, and it was able to reduce its energy costs by 10%.

4. Collaboration and communication: AI can also be used to enhance collaboration and communication in project and program management. AI systems can be used to facilitate real-time communication and collaboration between project and program team members, which can help to improve coordination and reduce misunderstandings. This can be particularly important in projects and programs with large and geographically dispersed teams.

For example, a global engineering firm used an AI system to facilitate communication and collaboration between its team members. The AI system was able to provide real-time updates on project progress and status, and it was able to connect team members through video conferencing and messaging. As a result, the company was able to improve its project delivery times by 20%, and it was able to reduce its communication costs by 30%.

In conclusion, AI has the potential to greatly benefit project and program management, and there are many ways that AI can be used to improve efficiency, productivity, and decision-making in project and program management. By using AI for project scheduling and resource allocation, risk management, resource optimization, and collaboration and communication, project and program managers can improve their overall success and reduce the risk of cost overruns and delays.

CHAPTER 8

The use of AI in the world of Finance

In the world of finance industry there are many ways that AI can be used to improve efficiency, productivity, and decision-making. In this chapter, we will explore some of the ways that AI can be used in finance, and I will provide a few examples of how these techniques can be used in practice.

1. **Fraud detection and prevention:** One way that AI can be used in finance is in fraud detection and prevention. AI systems can be used to analyze large amounts of data and identify patterns and anomalies that may indicate fraudulent activity. This can help financial institutions to quickly and accurately identify and investigate potential fraud cases, which can help to reduce losses and improve security.

For example, a large bank used an AI system to analyze transaction data and identify potential fraud cases. The AI system was able to identify patterns and anomalies that indicated fraudulent activity, and it was able to alert the bank's fraud investigators to potential cases. As a result, the bank was able to prevent millions of dollars in losses, and it was able to improve its overall security and risk management.

2. Risk management: Another way that AI can be used in finance is in risk management. AI systems can be used to analyze large amounts of data and identify potential risks and vulnerabilities, which can help financial institutions to take proactive steps to mitigate those risks. This can help to improve the overall financial stability of financial institutions and reduce the risk of losses.

For example, a large insurance company used an AI system to analyze data on weather patterns and natural disasters. The AI system was able to identify potential risks and vulnerabilities, such as areas that may be particularly susceptible to flooding or hurricanes. As a result, the insurance company was able to adjust its underwriting and pricing policies to reflect these risks, which helped to improve its financial stability and reduce its losses.

3. Portfolio optimization: Another way that AI can be used in finance is in portfolio optimization. AI systems can be used to analyze data on financial markets and identify opportunities for portfolio optimization, which can help investors to maximize returns and minimize risk. This can help investors to make more informed investment decisions, and it can also help to improve the overall performance of their portfolios.

For example, a large asset management firm used an AI system to analyze data on financial markets and identify opportunities for portfolio optimization. The AI system was able to identify potential investment opportunities, such as undervalued stocks or bonds, and it was able to provide recommendations for how the firm could optimize its portfolio to take advantage of those opportunities. As a result, the firm was able to improve its investment returns and reduce its risk.

4. Customer service: AI can also be used in finance to improve customer service. AI systems can be used to provide real-time support and assistance to customers, which can help to improve customer satisfaction and reduce the workload of human customer service representatives.

For example, a large bank used an AI system to provide real-time support and assistance to its customers. The AI system was able to answer common customer questions, such as account balances and transaction history, and it was able to provide real-time support for more complex issues, such as loan applications and dispute resolution. As a result, the bank was able to improve its customer satisfaction rates and reduce its customer service costs.

In conclusion, AI has the potential to greatly benefit the finance industry, and there are many ways that AI can be used to improve efficiency, productivity, and decision-making in finance. By using AI for fraud detection and prevention, risk management, portfolio optimization, and customer service, financial institutions can improve their overall performance and reduce the risk of losses.

CHAPTER 9

The Use of AI in the Compliance arena

Corporate compliance refers to the process of ensuring that a company is in compliance with all applicable laws, regulations, and policies. This can include a wide range of areas, such as financial reporting, environmental protection, data privacy, and anti-corruption. Corporate compliance is important for several reasons. In this chapter, we will explore some of the ways that AI can be used to improve corporate compliance, and we will provide examples of how these techniques have been used in practice.

1. **Risk assessment:** One way that AI can be used for corporate compliance is in risk assessment. AI systems can

be used to analyze data on regulatory requirements and business operations, and they can be trained to identify potential risks and vulnerabilities. This can help companies to take proactive steps to mitigate those risks and improve their overall compliance.

For example, a large pharmaceutical company used an AI system to analyze data on regulatory requirements and its operations. The AI system was able to identify potential risks and vulnerabilities, such as data privacy violations and environmental impact, and it was able to provide recommendations for how the company could mitigate those risks. As a result, the company was able to improve its overall compliance and reduce its regulatory fines.

2. **Monitoring and surveillance:** Another way that AI can be used for corporate compliance is in monitoring and surveillance. AI systems can be used to analyze data on company operations, such as financial transactions and communications, and they can be trained to identify potential violations of regulations or company policies. This can help companies to quickly and accurately identify and investigate potential violations, which can help to improve their overall compliance and reduce the risk of legal and reputational damage.

For example, a large retail company used an AI system to monitor and surveillance its financial transactions. The AI system was able to identify potential violations of financial regulations, such as money laundering and insider trading, and it was able to alert the company's compliance team to potential cases. As a result, the company was able to quickly and accurately investigate potential violations, and it was able to reduce its legal and reputational risks.

3. **Training and education:** AI can also be used for training and education in corporate compliance. AI systems can be used to create interactive and immersive training programs, which can help employees to better understand regulatory requirements and company policies. This can help to improve overall compliance, and it can also help to reduce the risk of violations.

For example, a large financial services company used an AI system to create an interactive and immersive training program on data privacy regulations. The training program used virtual reality to simulate real-world scenarios, and it allowed employees to practice making decisions in compliance with the regulations. As a result, the company was able to improve its overall compliance and reduce its risk of data privacy violations.

In conclusion, AI has the potential to greatly benefit corporate compliance measures. By using AI for risk assessment, monitoring and surveillance, and training and education, companies can improve their overall compliance, reduce their legal and reputational risks, and improve their overall performance.

CHAPTER 10

Disparity Studies utilizing AI

Artificial Intelligence (AI) can be a valuable tool for conducting disparity studies, which are used to analyze the impact of government programs and policies on different racial and ethnic groups. In this chapter, we will explore some of the ways that AI can be used for disparity studies, and we will provide examples of how these techniques have been used in practice.

1. **Data analysis:** One way that AI can be used for disparity studies is in data analysis. AI systems can be used to analyze large amounts of data on government programs and policies, and they can be trained to identify patterns and trends that may indicate disparities. This can help researchers to better understand the impact of government

programs and policies on different racial and ethnic groups, and it can help to inform policy decisions.

For example, a research organization used an AI system to analyze data on government housing programs. The AI system was able to identify patterns and trends that indicated disparities in access to housing, such as differences in wait times and approval rates for different racial and ethnic groups. As a result, the research organization was able to provide insights to policy makers on how to improve housing equity.

2. Predictive modeling: Another way that AI can be used for disparity studies is in predictive modeling. AI systems can be used to create models that predict the impact of government programs and policies on different racial and ethnic groups, based on historical data and trends. This can help researchers to anticipate potential disparities, and it can help to inform policy decisions.

For example, a research organization used an AI system to create a model that predicted the impact of a proposed transportation policy on different racial and ethnic groups. The model was based on historical data on transportation patterns and demographics, and it was able to predict potential disparities in access to transportation services. As a result, the research organization was able to provide insights to policy makers on how to improve transportation equity.

3. **Geospatial analysis:** AI can also be used for geospatial analysis in disparity studies. Geospatial analysis uses data on location to analyze disparities, such as differences in access to resources and opportunities in different neighborhoods. This can help researchers to better understand the impact of government programs and policies on different racial and ethnic groups, and it can help to inform policy decisions.

For example, a research organization used an AI system to analyze data on access to grocery stores in different neighborhoods. The AI system was able to identify patterns and trends that indicated disparities in access to fresh food, such as differences in the number and location of grocery stores in different racial and ethnic neighborhoods. As a result, the research organization was able to provide insights to policy makers on how to improve food equity.

In conclusion, AI can be a valuable tool for conducting disparity studies. By using AI for data analysis, predictive modeling, and geospatial analysis, researchers can better understand the impact of government programs and policies on different racial and ethnic groups, and they can provide insights to policy makers on how to improve equity and fairness.

CHAPTER 11

AI Equity Audits

An AI equity audit is a process of analyzing the impact of AI systems on different racial and ethnic groups. AI equity audits are used to identify and address disparities in the use and impact of AI systems, and they can help to ensure that AI is developed and used in a way that is fair and equitable for all. Artificial Intelligence (AI) can be a valuable tool for conducting AI equity audits, which are used to analyze the impact of AI systems on different racial and ethnic groups.

In this chapter, we will explore some of the ways that AI can be used to conduct AI equity audits, and we will provide examples of how these techniques have been used in practice.

1. **Data analysis:** One way that AI can be used for AI equity audits is in data analysis. AI systems can be used to analyze large amounts of data on AI systems, such as data on user demographics, system performance, and outcomes. This can help researchers to better understand the impact of AI systems on different racial and ethnic groups, and it can help to inform policy decisions.

For example, a research organization used an AI system to analyze data on a facial recognition system. The AI system was able to identify patterns and trends that indicated disparities in accuracy and fairness, such as differences in error rates for different racial and ethnic groups. As a result, the research organization was able to provide insights to policy makers on how to improve the equity and fairness of the facial recognition system.

2. **Predictive modeling:** Another way that AI can be used for AI equity audits is in predictive modeling. AI systems can be used to create models that predict the impact of AI systems on different racial and ethnic groups, based on historical data and trends. This can help researchers to anticipate potential disparities, and it can help to inform policy decisions.

For example, a research organization used an AI system to create a model that predicted the impact of an autonomous vehicle system on different racial and ethnic groups. The model was based on historical data on transportation patterns and demographics, and it was able to predict potential disparities in access to transportation services. As a result, the research organization was able to provide insights to policy makers on how to improve transportation equity.

3. **Geospatial analysis:** AI can also be used for geospatial analysis in AI equity audits. Geospatial analysis uses data on location to analyze disparities, such as differences in access to resources and opportunities in different neighborhoods. This can help researchers to better understand the impact of AI systems on different racial and ethnic groups, and it can help to inform policy decisions.

For example, a research organization used an AI system to analyze data on access to AI services in different neighborhoods. The AI system was able to identify patterns and trends that indicated disparities in access to AI services, such as differences in the availability and affordability of AI services in different racial and ethnic neighborhoods. As a result, the research organization was able to provide insights to policy makers on how to improve AI equity.

In conclusion, AI can be a valuable tool for conducting AI equity audits. By using AI for data analysis, predictive modeling, and geospatial analysis, researchers can better understand the impact of AI systems on different racial and ethnic groups, and they can provide insights to policy makers on how to improve equity and fairness.

CHAPTER 12

The Use of AI for Research and Development

Research and development (R&D) refers to the process of creating new knowledge and products through scientific research, experimental development, and innovation. R&D is important for several reasons. First, it is a key driver of economic growth and competitiveness. New products and technologies created through R&D can help companies to enter new markets, improve their existing products and services, and create new revenue streams.

Second, R&D can help to address global challenges, such as climate change, healthcare, and energy security. Third, R&D can help to improve the quality of life for individuals and communities, through the development of new technologies and solutions for everyday problems. R&D typically involves a range of activities, such as basic research, applied research, and experimental development.

Basic research is focused on expanding knowledge in a particular field, such as through the study of fundamental scientific principles. Applied research is focused on applying existing knowledge to practical problems, such as through the development of new products or technologies. Experimental development is focused on testing and refining new products or technologies, and bringing them to market.

Artificial Intelligence (AI) can be a valuable tool for assisting with research and development (R&D) in a variety of fields. In this chapter, we will explore some of the ways that AI can be used to support R&D, and we will provide examples of how these techniques have been used in practice.

1. Data analysis: One way that AI can be used for R&D is in data analysis. AI systems can be used to analyze large amounts of data, such as scientific literature, patents, and research articles, and they can be trained to identify patterns and trends that may be relevant to a particular research project. This can help researchers to quickly and accurately identify relevant information, and it can help to improve the efficiency and productivity of the R&D process.

For example, a research organization used an AI system to analyze data on scientific literature. The AI system was able to identify patterns and trends in the literature that were relevant to the organization's research, and it was able to provide recommendations for potential areas of research. As a result, the research organization was able to improve its efficiency and productivity, and it was able to make more informed research decisions.

2. Predictive modeling: Another way that AI can be used for R&D is in predictive modeling. AI systems can be used to create models that predict the impact of different variables on a particular outcome, such as the effectiveness of a new drug or the performance of a new technology. This can help researchers to make more informed decisions about which research projects to pursue, and it can help to improve the overall success of the R&D process.

For example, a pharmaceutical company used an AI system to create a model that predicted the effectiveness of a new drug. The model was based on historical data on the drug's chemical structure and biological activity, and it was able to predict the drug's effectiveness in different patient populations. As a result, the company was able to make more informed decisions about which research projects to pursue, and it was able to improve the overall success of its R&D efforts.

3. **Automation:** AI can also be used for automation in R&D. AI systems can be used to automate repetitive and time-consuming tasks, such as data entry and image processing, which can save researchers time and resources. This can help to improve the efficiency and productivity of the R&D process, and it can also help to reduce the risk of errors.

For example, a research organization used an AI system to automate data entry for a large study. The AI system was able to quickly and accurately enter data from research participants, which saved the organization time and resources. As a result, the organization was able to improve its efficiency and productivity, and it was able to reduce the risk of errors.

In conclusion, AI can be a valuable tool for assisting with R&D in a variety of fields. By using AI for data analysis, predictive modeling, and automation, researchers can improve their efficiency and productivity, make more informed decisions, and reduce the risk of errors.

CHAPTER 13

The Use of AI for Public Policy and Legislation

In the arena of Public Policy and Legislation Artificial Intelligence (AI) has the potential to greatly benefit government legislation and policy, and there are many ways that AI can be used to improve the efficiency, effectiveness, and fairness of government processes. In this chapter, we will explore some of the ways that AI can be used for government legislation and policy, and we will provide examples of how these techniques have been used in practice.

1. **Policy analysis:** One way that AI can be used for government legislation and policy is in policy analysis. AI systems can be used to analyze large amounts of data and

identify patterns and trends that may be relevant to a particular policy issue. This can help policymakers to make more informed decisions about which policies to pursue, and it can help to improve the overall effectiveness of government policy.

For example, a government agency used an AI system to analyze data on crime rates and demographic trends. The AI system was able to identify patterns and trends that indicated potential policy interventions, such as targeted policing strategies or social programs. As a result, the agency was able to make more informed decisions about which policies to pursue, and it was able to improve the overall effectiveness of its crime reduction efforts.

2. Predictive modeling: Another way that AI can be used for government legislation and policy is in predictive modeling. AI systems can be used to create models that predict the impact of different policies on a particular outcome, such as the effect of a new tax policy on economic growth or the impact of a new environmental regulation on air quality. This can help policymakers to make more informed decisions about which policies to pursue, and it can help to improve the overall effectiveness of government policy.

For example, a government agency used an AI system to create a model that predicted the impact of a proposed tax policy on economic growth. The model was based on historical data on economic trends and tax policies, and it was able to predict the potential impact of the proposed policy on economic growth. As a result, the agency was able to make more informed decisions about the policy, and it was able to improve the overall effectiveness of its economic development efforts.

3. **Data analysis and visualization:** AI can also be used for data analysis and visualization in government legislation and policy. AI systems can be used to analyze large amounts of data and present it in a clear and accessible way, which can help policymakers to better understand complex issues and make more informed decisions.

For example, a government agency used an AI system to analyze data on energy consumption patterns and present it in a visual format. The visualization showed how energy consumption varied by time of day and by location, and it helped the agency to identify potential policy interventions, such as energy conservation programs or smart grid technology. As a result, the agency was able to make more informed decisions about its energy policy, and it was able to improve the overall efficiency and effectiveness of its energy programs.

4. Automation and streamlining: AI can also be used for automation and streamlining in government legislation and policy. AI systems can be used to automate repetitive and time-consuming tasks, such as data entry and document review, which can save government agencies time and resources. This can help to improve the efficiency and effectiveness of government processes, and it can also help to reduce the risk of errors.

For example, a government agency used an AI system to automate data entry for a large regulatory compliance program. The AI system was able to quickly and accurately enter data from regulatory filings, which saved the agency time and resources. As a result, the agency was able to improve its efficiency and effectiveness, and it was able to reduce the risk of errors.

In conclusion, AI has the potential to greatly benefit government legislation and policy. By using AI for policy analysis, predictive modeling, data analysis and visualization, and automation and streamlining, government agencies can improve their efficiency, effectiveness, and fairness. These techniques can help policymakers to make more informed decisions, improve the overall effectiveness of government policy, and reduce the risk of errors.

CHAPTER 14

How does AI and BlockChain work together

AI and blockchain technology have the potential to significantly improve the efficiency, security, and transparency of government operations. Some examples of how AI and blockchain can assist the government include:

1. **Fraud detection:** AI can be used to analyze large amounts of data and identify patterns and anomalies that may indicate fraudulent activity, reducing the risk of fraud and waste in government programs. Blockchain can also provide a secure and transparent record of transactions, making it easier to trace and investigate fraudulent activity.

AI can be used to assist with fraud detection in several ways, including:

A. Anomaly detection: AI can be used to analyze large amounts of data and identify patterns and anomalies that may indicate fraudulent activity. This can include analyzing transaction data, monitoring account activity, and identifying unusual behavior patterns.

B. Machine learning: AI can be trained to recognize patterns and trends that are indicative of fraudulent activity, allowing for more accurate and efficient fraud detection. Machine learning algorithms can be used to analyze historical data and identify patterns that may indicate fraud, such as unusual payment patterns or unusual account activity.

C. Natural language processing: AI can be used to analyze text data, such as emails or chat messages, to identify patterns and trends that may indicate fraudulent activity. This can include analyzing the language used in communications, identifying keywords or phrases that may indicate fraud, and flagging potential fraudulent communications for further investigation.

D. Image and video analysis: AI can be used to analyze images and videos, such as those from surveillance cameras or financial transactions, to identify patterns and trends that may indicate fraudulent activity. This can include analyzing the content of images and videos, identifying unusual behavior or patterns, and flagging potential fraudulent activity for further investigation.

E. Network analysis: AI can be used to analyze network data, such as IP addresses and network traffic, to identify patterns and trends that may indicate fraudulent activity. This can include analyzing the behavior of individual users on a network, identifying unusual network activity, and flagging potential fraudulent activity for further investigation.

Overall, AI can be a powerful tool for fraud detection, allowing for more accurate and efficient identification of potential fraudulent activity. By analyzing large amounts of data and identifying patterns and trends, AI can help organizations to proactively detect and prevent fraud, ensuring that resources are used effectively and efficiently.

2. Cybersecurity: AI can be used to detect and prevent cyber attacks, protecting sensitive government data and ensuring compliance with data protection regulations. Blockchain can provide a secure and decentralized platform for storing and sharing data, reducing the risk of data breaches and ensuring data integrity.

Artificial Intelligence (AI) has the potential to greatly improve cybersecurity by helping businesses detect and prevent cyber threats, such as malware and phishing attacks. Here are five ways that AI can help with cybersecurity:

A. Anomaly detection: AI can be used to analyze network traffic and identify unusual patterns or behaviors that may indicate a security threat. This can help businesses quickly detect and respond to potential threats before they become more serious. For example, AI can be used to detect anomalous network traffic patterns that may indicate a malware infection or a phishing attack.

B. Threat intelligence: AI can be used to analyze threat data from a variety of sources, such as security reports and social media, to identify emerging threats and trends. This can help businesses stay ahead of potential threats and take proactive steps to protect their data and systems. For example, AI can be used to analyze social media posts and identify potential phishing scams before they are widely distributed.

C. Authentication and access control: AI can be used to improve authentication and access control by analyzing user behavior and identifying potential threats. This can help businesses ensure that only authorized users have access to sensitive data and systems. For example, AI can be used to analyze user login patterns and identify potential login attempts that may indicate a phishing attack or a compromised account.

D. Incident response: AI can be used to help businesses respond more quickly and effectively to security incidents. This can help businesses minimize the damage caused by a security breach and restore normal operations as quickly as possible. For example, AI can be used to analyze the impact of a security incident and prioritize the response efforts to address the most critical issues first.

E. Predictive analytics: AI can be used to analyze historical data and make predictions about future threats and vulnerabilities. This can help businesses take proactive steps to prevent security incidents before they occur. For example, AI can be used to predict which systems or applications are most at risk of a security breach and to prioritize security efforts to protect those areas.

It's worth noting that while AI has the potential to greatly improve cybersecurity, it's important to approach its use with caution. There are concerns about privacy and security with the collection and use of customer data, and it's important that businesses are transparent about how they are using AI and provide customers with control over their data. Additionally, there are concerns about bias and discrimination with AI algorithms, and it's important that these issues are addressed and mitigated to ensure that AI is fair and equitable for all users.

In conclusion, AI has the potential to greatly improve cybersecurity by helping businesses detect and prevent cyber threats. By leveraging AI, businesses can quickly identify potential threats, respond to incidents more effectively, and take proactive steps to prevent future threats. However, it's important to approach its use with caution and ensure that privacy, security, and fairness are prioritized. With proper consideration and implementation, AI can be a powerful tool for improving the cybersecurity of businesses.

3. Supply chain management: AI can be used to optimize supply chain operations and improve efficiency, reducing costs and improving delivery times. Blockchain can provide a secure and transparent platform for tracking and verifying the provenance of goods, ensuring compliance with regulations and reducing the risk of counterfeit goods entering the supply chain.

4. **Voting systems:** AI and blockchain can be used to improve the security and transparency of voting systems, reducing the risk of fraud and ensuring that every vote is counted accurately.

5. **Healthcare:** AI can be used to analyze health data and identify patterns and trends, improving the efficiency and effectiveness of healthcare services. Blockchain can provide a secure and decentralized platform for storing and sharing health data, ensuring patient privacy and improving the coordination of healthcare services.

Overall, AI and blockchain have the potential to significantly improve the efficiency, security, and transparency of government operations, while also reducing costs and improving the overall customer experience.

CHAPTER 15

The Modern Technology Trinity (AI, Blockchain and Cryptocurrency)

As we approach a new revolution in particular the 4th industrial revolution we have three major technologies Artificial Intelligence (AI), Blockchain, and Cryptocurrency which are three technologies that have the potential to greatly impact the future of finance and beyond. In this chapter, we will explore how these technologies work together and the potential benefits they can offer.

1. **AI and Blockchain:** AI and Blockchain are two technologies that can work together to improve the efficiency and security of financial transactions. AI can be used to analyze data on financial transactions and identify patterns and trends that may be relevant to fraud detection

or risk management. Blockchain can be used to create a secure and transparent record of those transactions, which can help to improve trust and confidence in the financial system.

For example, a financial institution could use AI to analyze data on customer transactions and identify potential fraud cases. The institution could then use Blockchain to create a secure and transparent record of those transactions, which could help to quickly and accurately investigate the fraud cases and take appropriate action. This could help to reduce the risk of financial losses and improve the overall security of the financial system.

2. AI and Cryptocurrency: AI and Cryptocurrency can also work together to improve the efficiency and security of financial transactions. Cryptocurrency is a digital or virtual currency that uses cryptography for security. AI can be used to analyze data on cryptocurrency transactions and identify patterns and trends that may be relevant to fraud detection or market analysis.

For example, a cryptocurrency exchange could use AI to analyze data on cryptocurrency transactions and identify potential fraud cases. The exchange could then use cryptography to secure those transactions and create a transparent record of them on a blockchain. This could help to reduce the risk of financial losses and improve the overall security of the cryptocurrency market.

3. **Blockchain and Cryptocurrency:** Blockchain and Cryptocurrency can also work together to create a decentralized and secure financial system. Blockchain can be used to create a secure and transparent record of cryptocurrency transactions, which can help to improve trust and confidence in the cryptocurrency market. Cryptocurrency can be used to facilitate transactions on the blockchain, which can help to reduce the need for intermediaries and improve the overall efficiency of the financial system.

For example, a group of individuals could use Blockchain and Cryptocurrency to create a decentralized financial system that allows for peer-to-peer transactions without the need for intermediaries. This could help to reduce transaction costs and improve the overall efficiency of the financial system.

In conclusion, AI, Blockchain, and Cryptocurrency are three technologies that have the potential to greatly impact the future of finance and beyond. By working together, these technologies can improve the efficiency, security, and transparency of financial transactions, and they can help to create a decentralized and secure financial system. These technologies can help to reduce transaction costs, improve trust and confidence in the financial system, and reduce the risk of financial losses.

CHAPTER 16

The Ethics of AI

During my travels I am often asked about the ethics of AI and the best thing I can do is explain it like this Artificial Intelligence (AI) is a very powerful and rapidly advancing technology, and it has the potential to greatly impact our lives and society. However, with this power comes a set of ethical challenges that must be addressed. In this chapter, we will explore some of the key ethical issues related to AI, and we will provide recommendations for how to address these challenges.

1. **Bias and discrimination:** One of the key ethical challenges related to AI is the risk of bias and discrimination. AI systems are trained on data, and if that data is biased or discriminatory, the AI system may also be biased or

discriminatory. This can have serious consequences, such as unfair treatment or discrimination in areas such as hiring, lending, and criminal justice.

To address this challenge, it is important to ensure that the data used to train AI systems is representative and unbiased. This may involve collecting data from a diverse range of sources, and it may involve using techniques such as data balancing or fairness metrics to ensure that the data is representative. It is also important to ensure that the AI systems themselves are designed to be fair and equitable, and to provide mechanisms for users to report and address any instances of bias or discrimination.

2. Privacy and surveillance: Another ethical challenge related to AI is the risk of privacy and surveillance. AI systems can be used to collect and analyze large amounts of data, which can include sensitive personal information. This can raise concerns about data privacy and security, and it can also raise concerns about the potential for surveillance and monitoring.

To address this challenge, it is important to establish clear guidelines and policies for the collection and use of personal data. This may involve obtaining informed consent from individuals before collecting their data, and it may involve using techniques such as anonymization or pseudonymization to protect individuals' privacy. It is also important to ensure that AI systems are designed to be transparent and accountable, and to provide mechanisms for individuals to access and control their data.

3. **Accountability and transparency:** Another ethical challenge related to AI is the risk of accountability and transparency. AI systems can be complex and difficult to understand, and it can be challenging to identify who is responsible for their actions and decisions. This can raise concerns about accountability and responsibility, and it can also raise concerns about the potential for misuse or abuse of AI systems.

To address this challenge, it is important to ensure that AI systems are designed to be transparent and accountable. This may involve providing detailed explanations of how the AI system works, and it may involve providing mechanisms for users to report and address any instances of misuse or abuse. It is also important to establish clear guidelines and policies for the use of AI systems, and to ensure that there are mechanisms for holding individuals and organizations accountable for their actions and decisions.

4. Human oversight and control: Another ethical challenge related to AI is the risk of human oversight and control. AI systems can be powerful and autonomous, and it can be challenging to ensure that they are being used in a way that aligns with human values and goals.

To address this challenge, it is important to establish clear guidelines and policies for the use of AI systems, and to ensure that there are mechanisms for human oversight and control. This may involve establishing human-in-the-loop systems, where humans are involved in the decision-making process, or it may involve establishing clear lines of accountability, compliance and responsibility for AI systems. It is also important to ensure that AI systems are designed to be adaptable and flexible, and to allow for human intervention and oversight when necessary.

In conclusion, AI is a powerful and rapidly advancing technology, and it has the potential to greatly impact our lives and society. However, with this power comes a set of ethical challenges that must be addressed by all of us. By ensuring that AI is trained on unbiased data, that personal data is protected, that AI systems are transparent and accountable, and that there is always human oversight and control, we can help to ensure that AI is used in a way that aligns with human values and goals, and that it is used to benefit all of society at large.

Closing Chapter

Now that I have shown what AI is, what it entails and how it can be used not only for individuals and businesses and business operations. In conclusion, the Doorway to Your Success with Artificial Intelligence is a comprehensive guide to understanding and leveraging the power of AI to achieve personal and professional success. Throughout this book, we have explored the different ways that AI can be used to improve efficiency, productivity, and decision-making in a wide range of fields, from finance and healthcare to education and government.

We have also discussed the ethical challenges related to AI, and we have provided recommendations for how to address these challenges. By ensuring that AI is trained on unbiased data, that personal data is protected, that AI systems are transparent and accountable, and that there is human oversight and control, we can help to ensure that AI is used in a way that aligns with human values and goals, and that it is used to benefit all of society.

In the closing of this book, we would like to encourage readers to embrace the opportunities that AI presents, and to approach it with a sense of curiosity and excitement. AI is a powerful and rapidly advancing technology, and it has the potential to greatly impact our lives and society. By understanding how AI works, and by learning how to use it effectively, we can open up new opportunities and possibilities, and we can help to create a better future for ourselves and for the world.

So, we invite you to join us on this exciting journey, and to explore the Doorway to Your Success with Artificial Intelligence. With the right knowledge, skills, and attitude, you can unlock the full potential of AI, and you can use it to achieve your personal and professional goals. We wish you the best of luck on your journey, and we hope that you find this book to be a valuable resource as you explore the world of AI.

About Author

Dr. Demoine Kinney, is an organizational leader, strategist, business coach, and world renowned speaker among his many other talents. He has inspired countless clients worldwide to overcome limited belief systems and to discover their own untapped talents and infinite potential.

Dr. Kinney's extraordinary story of transforming his own life from disabled veteran struggling with PTSD to leading a multimillion dollar enterprise is the inspiration behind his bold mission to teach others that it is possible to do the same.

In addition, he has led, and supported multi-state organizations, administered policy and quality compliance for over 4000 personnel in 18 locations to ensure compliance with regulations and standards. Among these, he was responsible for nine networks worth $20B.

Dr. Kinney has spearheaded strategic planning and the launch of new technology; generated policies for capturing, processing, and transmission of information to ensure DOD utilized programs and services effectively. He's an results-driven management professional with a solid history of government and private sector for program development . Dr. Kinney uses stellar interpersonal and communication skills to build client relations, convey information to teams, and leadership. He extends his skills to consult, develop, and train entrepreneurs.

Among many prestigious awards and honors bestowed upon him, Dr. Kinney holds numerous college degrees which consist of a Doctorate in Metaphysics, Masters in Divinity, Bachelors of Science in Information Technology Management, BA in Biblical Counseling and an Associates of Applied Science in Information Systems Technology.

Today, clients worldwide revere Dr. Kinney for his mastery of teaching people how to accomplish unfathomable goals and tap their own limitless potential with courage and determination.

Made in the USA
Monee, IL
04 November 2026

67376112R00056